CONTENTS

1 - DOGS' EYES

What do you know about our eyes?

Owners who want to better understand their canine companions must recognize that dogs see the world from a different visual perspective. The differences begin with the structure of the eye. We have a good idea what dogs see because we know the make-up of the retina of a dog's eye.

The retina is the light sensitive portion of the eye. This structure is located in the back of the inside of the eyeball. The retina contains two types of light sensitive cells; rods and cones. Cones provide color perception and detailed sight, while rods detect motion and vision in dim light. Dogs have rod-dominated retinas that allow them to see well in the dark. Along with superior night vision, dogs have better motion visibility than humans have. However, because their retinas' contain only about one-tenth the concentration of cones (that humans have), dogs do not see colors as humans do.

While their color vision is somewhat limited and different than ours, they do see color, and a look at the world through a dog's eyes can provide insight into how they perceive the world.

Humans see the world in color because we (usually) have three types of color receptor cells, or cones, in our eyes. These are sensitive individually to red, green, and blue light, and the different intensities and proportions of those three colors as seen by our eyes are put together by the brain to create the full-color world as we know it.

Some humans, however, are colorblind, which is a generic term for various changes in color perception, depending upon which of the receptors are defective. Two of the more common types are red-green and blue-yellow, in which a person cannot distinguish the two colors named.

For dogs, their color vision is most similar to a human with red-green color blindness, although there are other differences. Dogs are less sensitive to variations in gray shades than humans are, as well as only about half as sensitive to changes in brightness.

So, the next time your dog can't find the red ball that you just threw onto a green lawn, remember that their world, while still full of vivid blues and yellows, is probably a bit less colorful than your own. But don't feel sorry for dogs because of this. What they lack in visual ability, they make up for in sense of smell. Their noses have been estimated to be up to 100 million times more sensitive than yours. Their eyesight may be limited, but they can smell in 3D, IMAX, and TechnicolorTM.

Dogs use other cues (such as smell, texture, brightness, and position) rather than relying solely on color. Seeing-eye dogs, for example, may not distinguish between a green or red stoplight; they look at the brightness and position of the light. This, along with the flow and noise of traffic, tell the dog that it is the right time to cross the street.

I know when I can be cross the street

How a dog's eyes are set determines the field of view as well as depth perception. Prey species tend to have eyes located on the sides of their head. This gives the animals an increased field of view and allows them to see approaching predators. Predator species, like humans and dogs, have eyes set close together. Human eyes are set straight forward while dog eyes, depending on the breed, are usually set at a 20 degree angle. This angle increases the field of view and therefore increases the peripheral vision of the dog.

Increased peripheral vision compromises the amount of binocular vision. Binocular vision occurs where the field of view of each eye overlaps. Binocular vision is necessary for depth perception. The wider-set eyes of dogs have less overlap and less binocular vision (thus less depth perception). Dogs' depth perception is best when they look straight ahead. This is not an ideal situation as their nose often interferes. Predators need binocular vision as a survival tool. Binocular vision aids in jumping, leaping, catching, and many other activities fundamental to predators.

In addition to having less binocular vision than humans have, dogs also have less visual acuity. Humans with perfect eyesight are said to have 20/20 vision. This means that we can distinguish letters or objects at a distance of 20 feet. Dogs typically have 20/75 vision. What this means is that they must be 20 feet from an object to see it as well as a human standing 75 feet away. Certain breeds have better visual acuity. Labradors, commonly used as seeing-eye dogs, are bred for better eyesight and may have vision that is closer to 20/20.

If you're silently standing across the field from your dog, don't expect him (her) to recognize you. He'll recognize you when you do some sort of motion particular to yourself. He (she) may also recognize your presence by his outstanding sense of smell and / or hearing. Because of the large number of rods in the retina, dogs see moving objects much better than they see stationary objects. Motion sensitivity has been noted as the critical aspect of canine vision. Much of dog behavior deals with posture and appropriateness. Small changes in your body posture mean a lot to your dog. Dog owners need to modify training based on this fact. If you want your dog to perform an action based on a silent cue, we suggest using a wide sweeping hand and arm motion in order to cue your dog.

When dogs go blind, owners often wonder if the dogs' quality of life has diminished to the point where they are no longer happy. Humans deal well with being blind, and humans are much more dependent on their eyes than are dogs. Blind dogs lead happy lives as long as they are comfortable. The owner may need to make some adjustments in the pet's environment. Some of these adjustments include fencing the yard, taking leashed walks, and not leaving unusual objects in the dog's normal pathways. Obviously, most blind dogs cannot navigate stairs very well. When blind dogs are in their normal environment, most people don't know they are blind.

Most dogs have brown eyes, but there are breeds with pale blue, speckled, golden or hazel colored eyes. Some dogs are odd-eyed, having one eye that is blue and another eye brown. The shape of the eye and its placement on the head varies with different breeds. Most are oval and placed midway between the side and front of their faces.

Dog fanciers have terms to describe certain eye colors and shapes:

- An eye that is clear blue but flecked with a white or lighter blue is known as a China Eye.
- Dogs with a prominent, visible third eyelid (nictitating membrane) are said to have Haw Eyes. Haw eyes are seen in such breeds as the St. Bernard and Bloodhound.
- Triangular eyes have a three cornered, tent shaped appearance and are seen in Afghan Hounds.
- Wall eyes, characterized by a pale bluish-white iris with flecks of brown, are seen in some Harlequin Great Danes.
- Prominent eyes are big, round projecting eyes such as seen on Pugs.

Other eye shapes include Almond, Circular and Oval.

Congratulations! Now you know what my eyes are!!

2 - WHAT CAN THEY SEE?

But, what can we see through our eyes?

1. **Dogs can see in much dimmer light than humans.** This is because the central portion of a dog's retina is composed primarily of rod cells that "see" in shades of gray while human central retinas have primarily cone cells that perceive color. The rods need much less light to function than cones do.

2. **Dogs can detect motion better than humans can.**

3. **Dogs can see flickering light better than humans.** The only significance to this appears to be that dogs may see television as a series of moving frames rather than as a continuous scene.

4. **Dogs do not have the ability to focus as well on the shape of objects (their visual acuity is lower).** An object a human can see clearly may appear to be blurred to a dog looking at it from the same distance. A rough estimate is that dogs have about 20/75 vision. This means that they can see at 20 feet what a normal

human could see clearly at 75 feet.

5. **Dogs are said to have dichromatic vision** -- they can see only part of the range of colors in the visual spectrum of light wavelengths. Humans have trichomatic vision, meaning that they can see the whole spectrum. Dogs probably lack the ability to see the range of colors from green to red. This means that they see in shades of yellow and blue primarily, if the theory is correct. Since it is impossible to ask them, it is not possible to say that they see these colors in the same hues that a human would. Whether or not the ability to see some color is important to dogs or not is hard to say.

Also consider the perspective that dogs see the world from. A dog with its eyes about 12 inches off the ground certainly sees the world a different way than a human with eyes about 48 inches off the ground like many 5th graders.

As humans we tend to think of dog's visual capabilities as inferior to ours. It is different but it may suit their needs better than possessing accurate color vision would.

Those things below are some interesting facts about us

6 FASCINATING FACTS ABOUT YOUR DOG'S EYES

Dogs don't see the same world we do. For them, things might look a little grainier and a lot less vibrant. Then again, dogs can also see things we can only dream about.

Here are six fascinating facts about your dog's vision, based on the texture of your dogs' eyes I said above.

1. DOGS SEE FEWER COLORS THAN WE DO

While scientists used to believe that dogs were color blind, turns out your dog can see colors, but with a different spectrum. "Dogs do have fewer color sensitive cone receptors in their retinas than their human counterparts," says Dr. Martin Goldstein, an integrative veterinarian and author of The Nature of Healing Animals. "In essence, this would make them similar to a person who is red-green color blind."

That doesn't mean dogs can't see red—it just doesn't look as vibrant to them. "That bright red toy has always looked a brown shade to them," says Dr. Gary Ryder, who works for VCA Southwest Michigan Animal Emergency and Referral Center. "This is why you may see a preferential treatment toward the blues and violets, as that is where the strength of their cones lies."

On the other hand, dogs' vision is more in tune with sepias and pastels than the full range that humans see, according to Ryder. "It has actually been reported that they can very accurately differentiate among different shades of gray, even though they would appear closely associated to us humans," Goldstein adds.

2. DOGS DON'T HAVE 20/20 VISION

When it comes to sharpness of vision, dogs don't fare as well as humans. A person with 20/20 vision can see what the average individual can see on an eye chart when he is standing 20 feet away. "When it comes to dogs, they are more in the 20/75 range," Ryder explains. "This means that the visual acuity that a dog sees at 20 feet is similar to what a human would see at 75 feet."

In human terms, the average dog would be considered somewhat nearsighted, Goldstein says. Think of it in terms of pixels, Ryder suggests. "If you remove 75 percent of the pixels in a normal clear image, that is what a dog would be seeing," Ryder says. "It's still clear, it's just more grainy than what we see."

3. DOGS HAVE A LARGER FIELD OF VISION

The field of view of the canine eye is usually 240 degrees, according to Ryder. "This is better than humans (180 degrees) and cats (200 degrees)," he says. However, this varies greatly between individual dogs and breeds.

"The wolf retina is the most sensitive to scanning a horizon and looking for predators/ prey," Ryder says. "A brachycephalic breed (Bulldogs, Pugs, Boxers, Boston Terriers) with forward-sitting eyes will see to the periphery better but they cannot see as well right in front of them."

4. DOGS CAN SEE MUCH BETTER AT NIGHT

While you probably already knew that cats can see really well in low light, the truth is that dogs can see almost as well as their feline friends. "Dogs and cats can see about seven times better in low or dim lights than people," Ryder says.

This is in part due to something called a tapetum at the back of the retina. "This is a reflective layer so light that is not absorbed by photoreceptors gets bounced back and forth in the back of the eye to give it another chance at being recognized," Ryder says. "Cats are especially good at this and they reflect 130 times more light than humans. This tapetum is what gives the glowing-eye look when you see a cat in the dark; that glow is light that is bouncing off the tapetum and then through the pupil and back to your eye."

5. DOGS HAVE A THIRD EYELID

While the third eyelid is an important part of your dog's eye, it's not technically used in vision.

The third eyelid (officially called the nictitating membrane) has a couple of functions. It is there, primarily, to protect the eye. "There is a very sensitive reflex called corneal reflex where any sensation on the cornea makes the third eyelid go up, outer eyelids close, and a muscle behind the globe pull the eye back," Ryder explains. The third eyelid also functions to produce tears, he adds.

6. DOGS' EYES CAN TELL YOU ABOUT THEIR HEALTH

One of the easiest health issues to detect through the eyes is liver disease. "With severe liver disease, a secondary condition occurs where there is retention of bile," Goldstein says. "This is commonly known as jaundice and probably the easiest place to detect this condition is a yellowing of the whites of the eyes."

On the other hand, a very pale sclera (the white outer layer of the eye) can be a sign of anemia from an abdominal bleed or kidney disease, according to Ryder.

In dogs, changes in the size of the pupil can also indicate a serious medical problem. "The pupils can be small when there is pain in the eye," Ryder says. "And two different sized pupils can be present with head trauma." The presence of blood in the space between the cornea and pupil can also indicate trauma or potentially rodenticide poisoning (rat bait).

A cloudy eye can indicate the presence of protein or white blood cells. "This can be secondary to trauma, infection, auto-immune disease, cancer (lymphoma especially), diabetes, and many other conditions," Ryder says.

3 - COMMON DOGS' EYE PROBLEMS

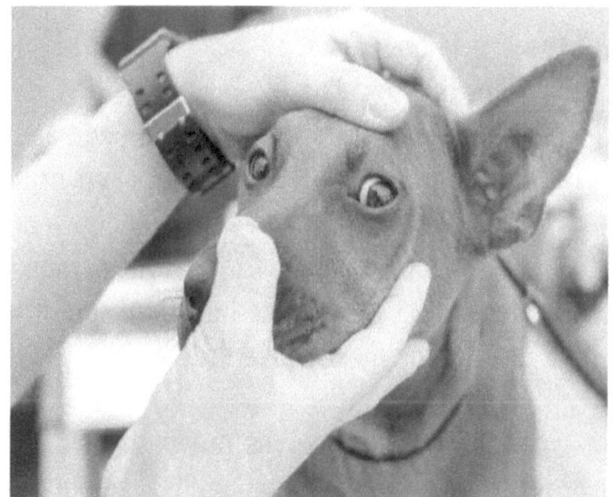

Ouch! I think I have something wrong in my eyes

A dog's eyes perform a nearly miraculous function – converting reflected light into nerve impulses that the brain uses to form images of the world. To do this well, all the various parts of the eye must be healthy. Unfortunately, a number of diseases can disrupt the way a dog's eyes function. Let's take a look at some of the most common eye problems dogs experience and how pet parents can manage them.

1. CHERRY EYE

Dogs have three eyelids – two that are readily visible and an extra one, called the third eyelid, that normally hides from view below the inner corner of the eye. The third eyelid is home to a tear producing gland. Normally, this gland is also invisible, but some dogs have a congenital weakness of the ligaments that hold it in place. When these ligaments fail, the gland pops out of its normal location and looks a bit like a "cherry" stuck at the inner corner of the eye. Because this condition often has a genetic basis, both eyes are usually affected over time.

To treat cherry eye, a veterinarian will perform a simple surgery to attach the gland back in a more normal position.

2. CORNEAL WOUNDS

The surface of the eye is covered with a clear, skin-like tissue called the cornea. Just like the skin, the cornea can be injured, and lacerations (cuts), punctures and ulcers are all quite common in dogs. Trauma is often to blame, like when a dog runs through tall grass and gets poked in the eye. In other cases, problems with the eyes themselves (like poor tear production or abnormal anatomy) can put dogs at risk for corneal damage. A dog with a corneal wound will often rub at the affected eye and squint because of pain. The eye may also be red and have excessive drainage.

Treatment for corneal wounds involves preventing or treating infections with antibiotic eye drops or ointments, managing pain and giving the cornea time to heal. In severe cases, surgery or other treatments may be needed to protect or repair the cornea and promote healing.

3. KERATOCONJUNCTIVITIS SICCA (KCS) OR DRY EYE

When dogs develop a disease called keratoconjunctivitis sicca (KCS) or dry eye, their tear glands produce fewer tears than normal. Tears perform important functions like removing potentially damaging material from the surface of the eye and nourishing corneal tissues. Unsurprisingly, a lack of tears can cause big problems including corneal ulcers, chronic drainage of mucus from the eyes and pain.

Mild cases of KCS can sometimes be managed with frequent application of an artificial tear solution, but medications that stimulate tear production (e.g., cyclosporine) are usually necessary. Surgery that redirects a duct carrying saliva so that it moistens the eye is an option in severe cases.

4. CONJUNCTIVITIS (PINK EYE)

The conjunctiva are the mucus membranes that cover the inside of a dog's eyelids, both sides of the third eyelid and some parts of the eyeball. "Conjunctivitis" or "pink eye" are interchangeable terms that simply mean "inflammation of the conjunctiva." The symptoms of conjunctivitis include reddened and swollen conjunctiva, eye drainage and discomfort.

Conjunctivitis should be thought of as a symptom of disease, not a disease itself. Many conditions cause conjunctivitis in dogs, including physical irritation (like dust and inward growing eyelashes), infections (bacterial and viral are most common) and allergic reactions. Treatment depends on the underlying cause. Sterile saline eye washes are available over the counter and can be used to flush irritants from the eye. Bacterial eye infections usually resolve quickly when treated with an appropriate prescription antibiotic eye drop or ointment. The chances of catching pink eye from your dog is very low but it only makes sense to wash your hands thoroughly after applying your dogs eye medications. Make a veterinary appointment if your dog's conjunctivitis worsens or fails to resolve over the course of a day or two.

5. GLAUCOMA

Within the eye, the production and drainage of fluid is precisely balanced to maintain a constant pressure. Glaucoma occurs when this balance is disrupted and pressure within the eye increases. Symptoms include pain, eye redness, increased tear production, a visible third eyelid, corneal cloudiness, dilated pupils and in advanced cases, an obviously enlarged eye.

Call your veterinarian immediately if you are worried that your dog might have glaucoma because delaying treatment can result in blindness. Treatment may involve a combination of topical and oral medications that decrease inflammation, absorb fluid from the eye, lower fluid production within the eye and promote drainage of fluid from the eye. Surgery may also an option in some cases.

6. CATARACTS

The lens is located in the middle of the eye and it is normally clear, but sometimes part or all of a lens develops a cloudy, opaque cataract. Cataracts block light from reaching the back of the eye resulting in poor vision or blindness, depending on their severity. Cataracts are often confused with a normal aging change that affects a dog's lenses called lenticular sclerosis. Both conditions give the pupils (the normally black center to the eye) a white, grey, or milky appearance, but a veterinarian can tell the difference through a standard eye exam.

Cataract surgery is available for dogs when their vision is severely compromised. If this is not an option, it is important to recognize that most dogs adapt very well to having poor vision.

7. ENTROPION

Some dogs have eyelids that roll inwards. This is called entropion. Entropion causes hair to rub on the surface of the eye, resulting in pain, increased tear production and eventually damage to the cornea. Entropion can be a congenital problem (dogs are born with it) or it can develop as a result of chronic squinting due to discomfort or eyelid scarring.

If entropion has occurred because of a condition that will resolve, a veterinarian can temporarily suture the eyelids into a more normal position (a procedure called eyelid tacking). Surgery to permanently fix abnormal eyelid anatomy is necessary in other cases.

8. PROGRESSIVE RETINAL ATROPHY (PRA)

Some eye diseases in dogs can be hard to spot. This is the case with progressive retinal atrophy (PRA), a condition that causes dogs to gradually become blind even though their eyes look quite normal. The first symptom of PRA is often difficulty seeing at night, but it is not unusual for dogs to behave normally until their eyesight is almost completely gone and/or they are taken to an unfamiliar environment.

Unfortunately, no effective treatment exists for PRA, but the condition is painless and dogs generally adapt extremely well to becoming blind.

REMEMBER: TALK TO YOUR VETERINARIAN

Of course there are many more conditions that cause eye problems in dogs than can be discussed here. Because eye problems have a tendency to worsen quickly, it is very important to discuss any concerns that you might have about your dog's eyes with your veterinarian as quickly as possible.

Woah, I'm looking at an amazing beauty!

4 - DOGS' NOSES

I've smelled something interesting

Of all the five senses, a dog's sense of smell is the most advanced. The nose is how a dog explores its world. On a walk, the dog gathers information about the neighborhood by smelling the grass, the trees, and the bushes. This information allows the dog to discover who has been in his neighborhood, where they are headed, their sex, their stature, and other vital details. With so much emphasis placed on the nose and the sense of smell, it is only fitting that the health of the nose be of the utmost importance. So, if a dog's nose is warm and dry, does that mean they are ill? Over the course of the day, the nose can range from cool and wet to dry and warm, and all are normal. This paper below will look into the intricacies of the dog's nose.

ANATOMY OF THE DOG NOSE

The dog's nose is an amazing organ specifically designed for detecting odors. An examination of the exterior and interior nose is necessary to fully understand and appreciate this remarkable structure.

The exterior nose of the dog dominates its face, extending from the stop to the tip of the nose. The rhinarium is the hairless, moist surface located around the nostrils (nares). The groove located down the center of the nose is the philtrum. The moist, hairless area of the nose displays a unique pattern of ridges and dimples. This area, along with the outline of the nostril openings, makes up the nose print. The nose print is thought to be unique and individual to each dog, similar to a human's fingerprint.

The two structures used for inhaling air and scents are the nostrils and the bony nasal cavity. The nasal cavity is divided into two chambers by the bony, cartilaginous nasal septum. The nasal cavities house the turbinate bones and paranasal sinuses.

The dog's nose is kept moist by lacrimal (tear) and nasal gland secretions. The moist nose allows the dog to inhale a larger number of scent molecules. Once the scent is captured, it is dissolved and transported to the olfactory (scent) region inside the nose. The olfactory receptor cells are located in this region. The number of cells present varies based on the length and size of the nose. For example, a Dachshund has 125 million scent cells while the German Shepherd & Beagle have 225 million. It is believed that the Bloodhound has the largest number of scent cells with about 300 million. Compared to dogs, humans have far less scent cells, only 5 million. In addition, dogs have fifteen times more cilia, hair like structures that capture scent, on their cells than humans.

Within the nasal cavity, is a series of scroll-shaped bony plates called turbinates. The turbinates are lined with specialized mucous membranes which contain the scent-detecting cells and olfactory nerves. The surface area covered by this structure, if unfolded, could stretch to approximately sixty square inches. In humans, the olfactory area is much smaller, only about the size of a postage stamp. Once the odor molecules are trapped in the olfactory region of the nose, they are absorbed into the mucous layer and diffused. The interaction converts the odor to a nerve impulse and the olfactory nerves transmit the message to the smell center of the brain. The dog's brain has a well-developed olfactory area which is dedicated to analyzing and interpreting odors. The dog's olfactory area in the brain is forty times larger than the area in the human brain.

Dogs have an additional olfactory cavity called the vomeronasal organ which is also lined with olfactory epithelium. This organ, known as Jacobson's organ, consists of two elongated fluid-filled sacs that open into the nasal cavity and oral cavity. Located in the bottom of the dog's nasal passage, Jacobson's organ detects pheromones. Pheromones are chemicals secreted in the urine by both sexes and are used to mark territory and provide information about mating readiness. The pheromone molecules detected by Jacobson's organ do not get mixed with the other odors and are analyzed by an area of the brain dedicated entirely to them.

EFFICACY OF THE DOG'S NOSE

Over the years, humans have grown to realize the importance of the dog's highly developed sense of smell and have employed dogs for many important tasks. Nowadays, it is not uncommon to hear of specially trained dogs performing assignments in the areas of search and rescue, bomb-sniffing, drugsniffing, weapons-sniffing, and detection of contraband food products. In addition, dogs have been used in homes to detect hazardous mold and locate termite infestations. Furthermore, researchers have discovered that dogs are able to detect some forms of cancer in humans, specifically, melanoma-types.

There are amazing true stories regarding the power of the dog's sense of smell. One drug-sniffing dog was able to detect marijuana in a plastic container which was submerged in a gas tank filled with gas. There is the two-year-old retriever that saved its nineteen-year-old human's life by detecting testicular cancer. The dog head butted its human in the groin causing serious swelling. When treated by a doctor, it was confirmed that he had stage two testicular cancer. There is also the story of the cancer-sniffing dog that insisted that a patient had melanoma, even after doctors stated they were cancer free. A second biopsy confirmed that a small amount of cells were melanoma cancer. There are several more stories like the ones above.

On the surface, your dog's nose may look wet, wriggling, and cute. But your pup's nose is actually a powerful device that guides him through his days in pretty impressive ways.

"Dogs noses are specifically adapted to function much better than ours," explains Michael T. Nappier, DVM, DABVP, of the Virginia Maryland College of Veterinary Medicine. "They have up to 300 million olfactory receptors in their noses, versus only about 6 million for us. And the part of their brain dedicated to interpreting these is about 40 times larger than ours."

Here are **six interesting facts about your dog's sense of smell** that prove canines have superior sniffers.

1. **A dog's nose has two functions—one for smell and one for respiration.** According to Nappier, a canine's nose has the ability to

separate air. A portion goes directly to the olfactory sensing area (which distinguishes scents), while the other portion is dedicated to breathing.

2. **Dog's also have the ability to take in and breathe out air at the same time.** "When sniffing, dogs noses are designed so that air can move in and out at the same time creating a continuous circulation of air, unlike humans who have to either breathe in or out only," says Nappier.

3. **Dog's have a special scent-detecting organ that humans don't have. This is called the vomeronasal organ,** says Nappier, and it helps canines detect pheromones, chemicals released by animals that affect other members of the same species. This organ plays an important role in reproduction and other aspects of canine physiology and behavior.

4. **Dogs smell in 3-D.** Dogs can smell separately with each nostril. Just as our eyes compile two slightly different views of the world, and our brain combines them to form a 3-D picture, a dog's brain uses the different odor profiles from each nostril to determine exactly where smelly objects are in the environment.

5. **A dog's nose has evolved to help them survive.** According to David C. Dorman, professor of toxicology at North Carolina State College of Veterinary Medicine, dogs have used their noses to assist with major life events since the beginning of time. "Evolutionarily, a dog's sense of smell helps them find a mate, offspring, food, and avoid predators," he says.

6. **Dogs can smell up to 100,000 times better than a human.** Nappier puts this tidbit into perspective with an awe-inspiring analogy. "A dog's sense of smell is its most powerful sense," he says. "It is so sensitive that [dogs can] detect the equivalent of a 1/2 a teaspoon of sugar in an Olympic-sized swimming pool."

WHICH DOGS HAVE THE BEST SENSE OF SMELL?

While all dogs have strong sniffers, Nappier says "hound breed dogs have the best sense of smell." Dorman points out that sturdy working dogs like German Shepherds and Labradors also rank high in their smelling abilities.

Some dogs, like Pugs who have short faces (also known as brachycephalic dogs), may "have some airway compromise that could affect their sense of smell," explains Nappier.

Are you guys talking about me?

5 - WHAT DOGS CAN SMELL

This flower is so fragrant!

Humans perceive the world through their vision, while dogs experience the world through their nose. Every smell is different for a dog, and each smell has a story behind it. When a dog smells a person, another dog, or any random scent, he is trying to determine the history behind it.

Dogs contain another special olfactory system above the roof of its mouth called the vomeronasal organ, which helps dogs sense things that they cannot see, such as human emotions. A dog can tell if a person is sad or happy, and this also helps dogs know whether an animal is friendly or dangerous to them. This unique ability also helps them identify potential mates.

The power of the canine sense of smell is unique and has helped humans in a number of ways. A dog can feel if a person is sick or sad, and can even identify if someone is pregnant. With proper training, some dogs can even be trained to detect bombs. They can sense the emotions of humans and react appropriately in a time of need, and they also have been able to help in the early detection of cancer in humans, essentially saving the lives of their owners.

A dog does not care how you look or dress, but if he gets good vibes from your smell, then a dog will love you. The world is truly a better place because of these wonderful creatures that we are lucky enough to welcome into our lives.

Why not make the world smell a bit more beautiful for them?

I'm sure you already know some things about a dog's incredible sense of smell, but I wonder if you realize all the things dogs can smell that are way beyond the scope of our human ability.

A dog's brain is specialized for identifying scents, and canines rely on their sense of smell to interpret their world much like we use our sight to interpret ours. The percentage of the dog's brain that is devoted to analyzing smells is actually 40 times larger than that of a human! It's been estimated that dogs can identify smells somewhere between 1,000 to 10,000 times better than humans can.

Inside a Dog's Nose

There are up to 300 million olfactory receptors in a dog's nose, allowing them to detect odors in parts per trillion. Compare that to a mere 5 million receptors in the human nose, with the ability to detect orders in parts per billion. The dog's sense of smell is thought to be 10,000 to 100,000 times more acute than ours.

Unbelievable Things Dogs Can Smell That Humans Cannot
Some Unbelievable Things Dogs Can Smell (that humans can't)

1. Cancer

Dogs trained to detect cancer have an accuracy rate between 88 and 97% versus machines, which is between 85 and 90%., by simply sniffing the a breath, urine, or blood sample.

2. Epilepsy

Seizure Alert Dogs can warn a person of an oncoming epilepsy attack anywhere from 15 minutes to 12 hours before. Some are trained to guard the owner, keeping them away from stairs, while others are trained to press a button on a phone to dial emergency services.

3. Computer Gear

Yes, computer gear, such as hard drives and other digital devices. These specially trained dogs are being used to find evidence child pornographers and other cyber criminals may have hidden away. (You can run, but you can't hide.)

4. Ovulation

Cows are most often impregnated via artificial insemination. But because bull semen is so expensive, many farmers can only afford to artificially inseminate the cows when they're definitely ready to get pregnant. Time it badly, and there would be an awkward conversation with the bank manager down the line. As a result, some farmers have started using specially-trained dogs to detect when a cow is in heat—a job some dogs are so good at, they even know before the bulls do.

5. Bed bugs

the modern age of widespread air travel is causing a near-apocalyptic surge in the number of cases of bed bug infestations. In response to this, pest control services have sprung up whereby—in exchange for a hefty fee—a dog will sweep a house for bed bugs, letting you know before you purchase a new property what sort of problems you might have to deal with. Apparently, the accuracy rate is as high as 96 percent.

6. Emotions

Dogs can smell changes in your hormones and body chemicals, thereby detecting your emotions, which explains how they know when you're feeling sad, fearful, or ill.

7. Bacteria

Dog detecting diseased beehivesIn case you didn't already know—the bees are dying. But dogs have come to save the day: since the 1970s, bee keepers have trained dogs to find diseased beehives before they have a chance to infect other, healthier swarms. The dogs can do this simply by tracking the scent of the bacteria that causes the disease known as "American Foulbrood"—a process which allows beekeepers to inspect up to 100 colonies in 45 minutes, rather than the two days it would take a human to do the same work.

8. DVDs

Dogs detecting DVDsDogs can be taught to detect the material polycarbonate, a key component of all DVD disks. They can thereby help to bust the massive DVD counterfeiting trade in places like Southeast Asia. Indeed, on their first raid, two of these dogs found a pile of pirated DVDs worth over $3 million. The success of this single raid managed to annoy the Malaysian DVD pirates so much that they offered a $30,000 bounty for the deaths of the dogs.

9. Drowned Bodies

Dog detecting drowned bodiesWater search dogs are often used by police in the USA to locate and recover drowned corpses. But how exactly could a dog smell a body through all that water? Well, the scent of drowned bodied is released into the water currents, which then end up being released into the air. The dogs—which can work either from the shore, from a boat, or even while swimming in the water—track this scent to its strongest point, the body itself.

10. Diabetes

We've recently seen how some dogs can predict the onset of a seizure. Dogs can also be trained to alert their diabetic owners whenever their blood sugar rises to dangerous levels. A few of them can even—in the case of a diabetic attack—run and fetch an insulin kit. If only they had opposable thumbs, perhaps they'd prep the syringe for us as well.5

11. Whale Poop

Whale poop is often analyzed by scientists to monitor the health of whales, as it often contains important information about their diet. But there's one problem: the poop sinks within half an hour of leaving the whale, meaning that scientists need to get their hands on it as soon as possible. For this reason, one group has started training dogs to detect the poop. The dogs can trace its scent from a distance of more than one mile (1.6 km), and lead scientists to the smelly treasure. When the dog has detected the whale waste, he points out the location to the boat captain by either leaning left or right, or twitching his left or right ear.

12. Minerals and Ores

Ore Sniffing DogThe government in Finland financed a program that taught dogs to detect valuable sulphide-containing rocks. When the rocks break apart, they release a smell not unlike rotting eggs, which the dogs can track easily. So easily, in fact, that, during one hunt a dog found a deposit of "great economic significance."2

Another Fun Fact – Your Dog's Noseprint

Your dog's nose has a pattern of ridges and dimples that, in combination with the outline of its nostril openings, make up a nose print believed to be as individual and unique as a human being's fingerprints. Companies even register nose prints as a way of identifying and helping to locate lost or stolen dogs, a system that is now being used by kennel clubs around the world.

TOP SMELLS DOGS HATE

A dog's sense of smell is completely different from a humans', so it is not surprising that we have different tastes when deciding which fragrances seem pleasant and which aromas we consider unbearable. For us, the smell of urine and feces are some of the smells that repel us most. For dogs, these smells provide them with information which is of great interest to them.

Many of the smells dogs hate are found in our homes, producing discomfort in our dog's nose, thus presenting our dog with an unpleasant environment.

1. CITRUS

Humans tend to love the smell of citrus. Not only is it a lovely natural reminder of summer, but it is an aroma which can last for a long time. Therefore, we as humans often tend to buy products that contain citrus for a lasting fresh environment. However, our furry companions do not agree and this is one of the smells that dogs hate most.

Remember dogs have a sense of smell 40 times more developed than humans. Therefore, if the smell of citrus is already intense for a human, imagine how strong the smell of citrus is for a dog. It is such a strong aroma it can cause irritation in the animal's respiratory tract, producing both an annoying and unbearable sensation.

Citrus fruits, such as lemon, orange or grapefruit, give off smells that dogs can't stand. But, the scents that dogs hate the most are those provided by essential oils made with this type of fruit. Oils are concentrated products that emit a much more intense odor than the fruit itself. Therefore, animals perceive an even stronger odor than they would with the actual food itself.

If you intend to use a citrus scent to prevent your dog from urinating in a certain area of the home (such as the carpet), we recommend that you use natural fruits and avoid placing any oils within their reach. The purpose of this technique is to prevent the animal from approaching that specific area, not to offer an unpleasant coexistence.

While there are smells you can use to keep dogs away, it is important they are not harmful. This article on toxic fruit ad vegetables for dogs may be helpful.

2. VINEGAR

Vinegar is another ingredient used as a home remedy to prevent a dog from urinating inside. Dogs hate the smell of vinegar. As with citrus fruits, the aroma of vinegar is so strong that it is somewhat unbearable for dogs. However, apple cider vinegar is actually beneficial for dogs. Therefore, depriving them 100% of it is also not advisable. We must learn how to use vinegar properly and know how often to apply it, so that our animal always remains as comfortable as possible.

Apple cider vinegar is highly effective in preventing your dog from smelling bad. However, since this is one of the scents dogs hate, we suggest mixing it with their usual shampoo to reduce its fragrance. Do not apply this solution to their head area and make sure to rinse them well after applying it.

3. CHILI

Chili, or chili pepper is a food that owes its hot taste to a series of natural chemical compounds called capsaicinoids. In humans capsaicinoids are used from everything to flavoring chili and even help reduce obesity[1]. Dogs, however, are incredibly repelled by the natural smell of chili. So much so, that smelling this food directly can cause respiratory irritation, itching in the nose and constant sneezing in a dog. It is therefore essential to know which human foods are banned for dogs to prevent them from consuming them.

4. ALCOHOL

Antiseptic alcohol is a smell dogs don't like. We completely discourage applying alcohol to a dog's skin. In case of injury, the best thing to do is to clean the wound with water and go to the vet so that he/she is the one to disinfect it. If you are in a situation in which you cannot go to a specialist, we recommend consulting the following article in which we discuss how to make natural disinfectant for dogs and apply it by following the instructions.

A dog's reaction to this will depend mostly on the alcohol content of the disinfectant. In addition to this, dogs hate antibacterial gel agents and some alcoholic beverages. This is not the case for all of them. A dog may try to drink a beer or a cocktail which it otherwise thinks is tasty. Remember, even if we cannot necessarily smell much, they can smell everything.

5. NAIL POLISH

The smell of nail polish can be pleasant for many people, but dogs detest this smell too. Nail polish is made up of a high number of chemical compounds, so it is not natural. They include formaldehyde, nitrocellulose, isopropyl alcohol and acetate. Dogs hate the smell of these fragrances. If a dog comes into contact with nail polish it can also cause them to sneeze and itch excessively.

On the other hand, nail polish removers also form part of the list of smells that dogs hate. This is due to their chemical compounds, the scent of acetone being perhaps the most annoying smell of all for dogs. We recommend opting for acetone-free nail polish remover and/or keeping all of these cosmetic products away from dogs.

6. CHLORINE AND CLEANING PRODUCTS

Although for us they produce a fresh and clean ambiance, dogs hate the smell of cleaning products. Not only do dogs not like this smell, but these products are also highly harmful and dangerous for dogs. Inhaling these chemicals directly can cause irritation of a dog's respiratory tract and esophagus. In addition, ammonia produces an aroma very similar to that released by a dog's urine. A dog will then associate this 'urine' smell to the presence of another animal at home and it can cause stress in dogs.

Although the above mentioned products are considered the most annoying products for dogs, they generally hate the smell of all cleaning products. Many cleaning products are given scents such as citrus which the dog would hate anyway. If you need to clean the house, we recommend trying to clean the house while another family member takes the dog for a walk. This will avoid placing your dog in an unpleasant environment. Enzymatic cleaners are the best to use if you have a dog in the house. Many don't even use scents, so they are unlikely to repel your pet.

IS NAPHTHALENE TOXIC FOR DOGS?

Yes, naphthalene is toxic for dogs. Naphthalene is generally used as a pesticide, due to its high level of toxicity. No only do dogs hate the smell of this chemical, but if ingested it can kill your dog. The ingestion of a single naphthalene ball can cause serious damage to a dog's liver and central nervous system. The result is vomiting, diarrhea and convulsions. You will need to take them to the vet to counteract this action, otherwise it could be fatal.

DO DOGS LIKE THE SMELL OF PERFUME?

No, dogs hate the smell of perfume. Have you ever noticed that, after perfuming yourself and trying to hug your dog, he or she rejects you? This is because perfumes are products made with a great amount of chemical compounds and scents that dogs hate.

In addition to the unpleasant smell, dogs also hate the smell of perfume because it camouflages the smell their owner's natural body odor, a smell that comforts them. Remember that dogs recognize us by our smell, if we hide it under another one, it is not surprising that they will naturally detest that unpleasant fragrance that prevents them from identifying us.

What about dog perfume? yes, dogs also don't like this smell. However, as long as they are of: good quality, are not harmful and are specifically manufactured for dogs, you can apply them in moderation.This means that we do not recommended putting perfume on your animal every day, but once in a while; as a canine hairdresser would.

As with humans, every animals has a taste of their own and therefore may not find all of the smells mentioned to be unpleasant. This is not an exact science and you might find that one dog likes the smell of something while another dog hates the same smell. But in conclusion, we can gather that anything that causes a citrus-y or chemical-type smell, should be avoided!

6 - DOGS' NOSE PROBLEMS

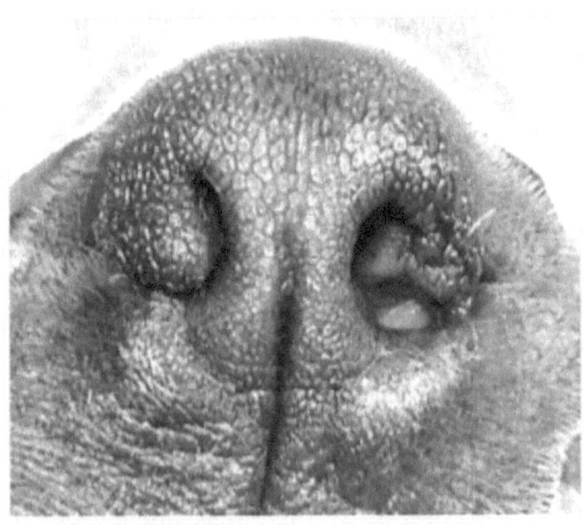

Something's not good right here!

1. ASPERGILLOSIS

This condition is the result of fungi (Aspergillus and penicillin species) that lives in leaf mulch or soil with the potential to colonize the dog's nasal chambers. Infection is most common in breeds with long noses, and the symptoms include nosebleeds, facial pain and a long-term nasal discharge that starts out straw-colored and rapidly becomes purulent.

Diagnosis can be made by running a special blood test or by imaging the nasal chambers to look for the fungal colonies. Treatment is essential; left unchecked, the fungi can destroy the bony scrolls inside the nose.

Oral therapy has a low success rate because the drugs struggle to reach a high-enough concentration in the nose to be effective. This makes nasal flushes with antifungals the dog's best chance of recovery.

2. CANCER

Happily, nasal cancer is rare in dogs. Those cancers most likely are squamous cell carcinoma of the leathery nose or osteosarcoma affecting the bony chambers inside the muzzle. In the first case, the nose becomes ulcerated and bleeds; in the second, the face becomes swollen.

Radiotherapy can be highly effective but requires anesthesia for each dose and is only available at certain oncology specialist centers.

3. DEPIGMENTATION

What's happening when that trademark black leather nose loses color and turns pink?

Strangely, rottweilers are most commonly linked to pigment loss in the nose. This can have many causes, including:
- Allergy to plastic food bowls (causing the immune system to be overactive and attack pigment cells)
- Immune-mediated conditions (pemphigus and lupus) where the body attacks its own cells
- Uveo-dermatological syndrome (linked to exposure to the sun)
- Vitiligo
- Rare cancers

Treatment involves identifying the reason and treating that.

4. FOREIGN BODY

A nose in full sniff exerts a powerful pull on small objects that are then sucked up into the nasal cavity. Hopefully, a few vigorous sneezes will eject it straight out again, but sometimes objects become stuck.

The signs include frantic pawing at the nose, sneezing and eventually a discharge from just 1 nostril. The vet may look up the nose with a fine camera, and then either flush the offending object out or use special graspers.

5. NASAL MITES

This microscopic mites' favored residence is the dog's nasal cavity, where it causes itching and irritation. Treatment includes the use of anti-parasite products from the ivermectin family.

6. NOSEBLEEDS

Nosebleeds, or "epistaxis," are a symptom rather than a diagnosis in their own right. They can result from damage to blood vessels in the nose as a result of infection, cancer or a foreign body. Also, dogs with blood clotting disorders (as a result of rat poison ingestion, lungworm infection or an inherited clotting problem such as Von Willebrand disease) may well suffer regular nosebleeds.

It's imperative to let the vet take a look and work up the problem to identify the root cause.

7. ORONASAL FISTULA

This is when a passageway opens between the mouth and nose (typically via the root cavity of a large canine tooth when it falls out or is removed). This allows food and drink to reflux up into the nose, where it sets up an infection. The treatment for this is reconstructive surgery to seal off the connecting channel.

8. REVERSE SNEEZING

Described as "choo-ahh," reverse sneezing mimics choking or coughing fits. It is extremely common and usually the result of an allergy or an overlong soft palate getting sucked into the windpipe. Most cases are self-limiting and respond to gently stroking the throat.

A few dogs may require steroids or antihistamines to settle an episode, and rarely corrective surgery is needed to trim back a long soft palate.

9. RHINITIS

This means inflammation of the nose, and the signs include a long-term nasal discharge and sneezing. The causes range from infections to allergies, but sometimes is never identified. Some dogs are long-term sufferers, which can be very frustrating for the human.

10. SNEEZING

Another symptom rather than a diagnosis, this can result from infection, irritation or allergy.

11. NASAL SKIN CONDITIONS

It is often said that a warm dry nose is a sign of illness; however, this is not always the case. If a dog exhibits other symptoms, such as changes in color (pigment loss) or changes in texture (flaky, cracked, lesions) the nose should be examined by a traditional or holistic veterinarian. There are several conditions that affect the skin on the nose of dogs. The area most frequently involved is the hairless, cobblestoned tip of the nose. An overview of the skin disorders follows.

12. NASAL HYPERKERATOSIS

With nasal hyperkeratosis, the outer layer of skin on the edges of the nose becomes thickened. The moist, soft surface of the nose gives way to a rough, hard, and dry surface, especially on the top of the nose. The nose may also become painful from the development of cracks, sores and erosions. Bacterial and yeast infections may develop in the cracks. Like many other nose related irritations, there is no known cause for nasal hyperkeratosis. However, it is most prevalent in older dogs, especially the American Cocker Spaniel, Basset Hound, Beagle, and English Springer Spaniel. The typical treatment consists of a topical application of corticosteroids and for the inflammation and infection antibiotics. Additional treatments involve carefully cutting and shaving away the excess keratin. Also, an application of topical salves and wet dressings may be utilized.

13. NASAL SOLAR DERMATITIS

Nasal solar dermatitis or Collie nose is most common in sunny regions such as California, Florida, and the mountains of the West. It is caused by a lack of pigment on the nose and prolonged exposure to ultraviolet rays. Initially, the skin of the nose appears normal except for the lack of black pigment. When exposed to sunlight, the skin on the border of the nose becomes aggravated. As sun exposure continues, the skin becomes weepy and crusty and the hair begins to fall out. In severe cases, the entire region of the nose becomes inflamed with open sores. The breeds normally affected are the Australian Shepherd, Collie, Shetland Sheepdog, and related breeds.

For treatment of nasal solar dermatitis, it is recommended to limit the dog's sun exposure between the peak hours of 9 a.m. and 3 p.m. It is also suggested that a sunscreen designed specifically for dogs (such as Doggles Pet Sunscreen and Epi-Pet Sun Protector Spray), with SPF 15 or greater, be used during outdoor activities. It should be applied 30 to 60 minutes before sun exposure and throughout the day. For nose irritation, an application of 0.5 to 1.0 percent hydrocortisone is advised.

14. NASAL DEPIGMENTATION

With nasal depigmentation or Dudley nose, the dark pigmentation on the nose is normal at birth, but gradually fades from black to brown. In some cases, the nose loses all pigmentation and becomes pinkish white. There is no known cause for nasal depigmentation, but is possibly a form of vitiligo. It tends to occur most often in the following breeds – Afghan Hound,

Doberman Pinscher, German Shepherd (white), Irish Setter, Pointer, Poodle, and Samoyed. Treatment for pigment loss is not necessary, since it is considered a cosmetic issue. However, the use of sunscreen, as discussed under nasal solar dermatitis, is recommended to protect the nose from exposure to ultraviolet rays.

A seasonal version of pigmentation loss, called snow nose, occurs in the winter months. The nose's dark color fades during winter and then darkens again in the spring and summer months. There is no known cause for snow nose, but two theories exist. One theory attributes the pigment loss to cold winter temperatures, while the second theory believes the increase in sun reflection from the snow is the culprit. Whatever the cause, the breeds typically affected by snow nose include the Bernese Mountain Dog, Golden Retriever, Labrador Retriever, and Siberian Huskie. The use of sunscreen is suggested to protect the nose from ultraviolet rays.

Another type of dermatitis that causes pigment interruption on the nose is plastic dish nasal dermatitis. Plastic dish nasal dermatitis is triggered from a chemical sensitivity to p-benzyl hydroquinone. As a dog eats from a plastic or rubber bowl, this chemical is adsorbed through the skin and disrupts the production of melanin. This causes dark pigment in the skin. Additionally, the skin of the nose may become irritated
and inflamed. Changing the water and food bowl to ceramic, stainless steel, or glass will alleviate the problem.

Discoid lupus erythematosus is a relatively common autoimmune skin disease in dogs. The nose experiences pigment loss and sometimes texture loss. Following the pigment loss, inflammation, sores and crustiness may appear. The breeds most often affected by lupus erythematosus are the Collie German Shepherd, German Shorthaired Pointer, Shetland Sheepdog, Siberian Huskie, and also crossbreeds.

HOLISTIC THERAPIES

Besides traditional treatments, holistic therapies can also provide relief to the above mentioned nasal conditions. For example, Bach Flower Essences can be used to help speed up the healing process and also assist with any emotional issues associated with the nasal condition. For skin eruptions, bathing the affected area with Crab Apple or Rescue Remedy can help alleviate the sores. In addition, Rescue Remedy Cream can be applied directly to the area to soothe and heal. Other natural creams and oils that can prove effective for soothing a dry cracked nose are vitamin E oil, shea butter, kukui nut oil, lanolin, and coconut oil.

Herbal remedies may also provide relief to a dog nose that is dry and cracked, cracked and ulcerated, or inflamed. Creams like Calendula ointment – with its anti-inflammatory, anti-bacterial, and anti-fungal properties – can be used to inhibit inflammation, prevent the spread of inflammation, lessen pain, soften crusty areas, and moisten and soothe the dry, cracked nose skin. Astragalus also has anti-inflammatory and anti-bacterial properties so it can be used as an ointment or a wash for the affected dog nose. In addition, Astragalus and Echinacea both contain immune boosting properties which strengthen the dog's resistance to infection and inflammation which is important for getting the dog balanced and back to health.

Acupuncture and acupressure are important holistic treatments that can be utilized to strengthen the dog's immune function. In traditional Chinese medicine (TCM), the nose, throat, and vocal cords are closely connected to the lungs. Therefore, many disorders of the dog's nose are treated through the Lung Meridian (LU 1-LU 11). This Meridian is located at the forward point of the shoulder and continues down the foreleg to the medial side of the dewclaw (digit 1) of the front paw (see below).

Large Intestine (LI) 4 and Large Intestine (LI) 11 are both responsible for clearing toxins from the body and increasing the production of white blood cells. These two immune balancing points (LI 4 and LI 11)
are also located on the foreleg. Hence, massaging the dog's forelegs from the shoulder to the toes will stimulate all the Lung points and the two Large Intestine points.

For specific conditions, a holistic veterinarian may recommend any combination of acupressure, herbal pills and tinctures, topical creams and teas, nutritional supplements, and dietary changes. Each is used to treat a certain aspect of the condition.

Massage is also of great value to the dog. However, direct massage on the area of the nose with open sores, eruptions, or blisters should be avoided. Regular massage to the other areas of the body increase blood and lymph circulation which aids waste removal and supplies necessary nutrients to the tissues. The massage will also help release tension, reduce pain, and allow for relaxation. Further, it restores balance to the dog and enhances their overall well-being.

The dog's nose is its greatest asset. Throughout the day the nose partakes in many activities, from sniffing, to breathing, to digging and nudging. It is not surprising that the skin of the nose can become dry, cracked, and irritated. Fortunately, this condition is rarely serious and can be treated naturally. Best of all, the functional capability of the nose is not impacted.

7 - DOGS' BRAINS

What are you going to do with me?

Odds are you don't look forward to spending time in a magnetic resonance imager–and with good reason. The clanging, coffin-like machine seems purpose-built for sensory assault. But you're not Ninja, a 3-year-old pit-bull mix, who trots into a lab at Emory University in Atlanta, catches a glimpse of the MRI in which she'll spend her morning and leaps happily onto the table.

Ninja is one of the few dogs in the world that have been trained to sit utterly still in an MRI (the little bits of hot dog she gets as rewards help) so that neuroscientist Gregory Berns can peer into her brain as it works. "What's it like to be a dog?" Berns asks, a question that is both the focus of his work and the thrust of his next book. "No one can know with certainty. But I think our dogs are experiencing things very much the way we do."

That is what we want to believe. Our love affair with dogs has been going on for 15,000 years, and there's no sign that it's flagging. About 44% of families in the U.S. include at least one dog, meaning a canine population of up to 80 million.

Most of the time, we give our dogs very good lives. We fancy that they understand us, and maybe they do: come home sad and they'll nuzzle your hand. They don't have language, but they communicate volumes–with their eyes, with their barks, with their entire expressive bodies. "Dogs pick up on all kinds of things," says Juliane Kaminski, director of the Dog Cognition Centre at the University of Portsmouth, in England. "A system has developed in which both species–ours and theirs–attend to each other's cues."

That's something we know intuitively, but science is pushing harder to understand it empirically. Canine-research facilities have been established around the world, in Hungary, Austria, Germany, Italy, Australia and elsewhere. In the U.S. alone, there are facilities at Duke, Tufts and Yale universities. The Association for Psychological Science (APS), which typically concerns itself with the well-being of humans, recently devoted an entire issue of its journal Current Directions in Psychological Science to the canine mind. The findings were often impressive: Dogs can count–sort of– learning to look at two boards with geometric shapes attached to them and choose the one that has more. They can read human faces–understanding the importance of using gaze to communicate and to direct our attention. They can excel at what is known as object permanence–understanding that when an object is out of sight, it has not vanished from existence. It takes humans a lot longer to learn such a basic truth of the world, which is why babies who toss food or a spoon from a high chair will so often not look down at the floor to try to find it.

Dogs may be better too than 3-to-4-year-old children at learning to ignore bad instructions. In a Yale study not reported in the APS journal, dogs and small children were given a box and taught to turn a lever to open the lid and get a treat. When the lever was rigged so that it was no longer needed, the dogs learned to ignore it and simply open the box. The children continued to turn the useless thing all the same. If dogs can beat us at this one small task, what other gifts may they be hiding?

INSIDE THE MINDS OF DOGS

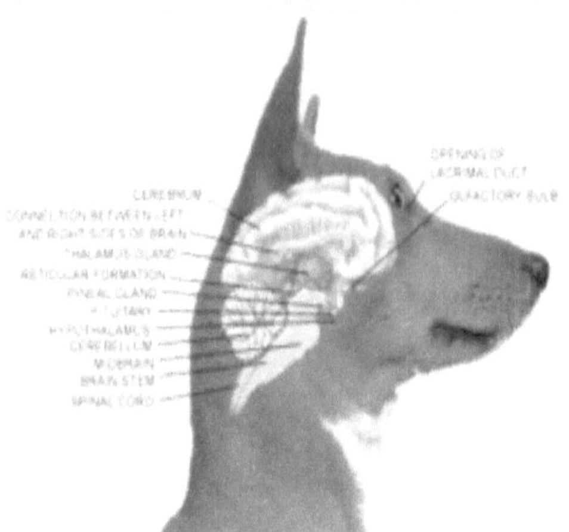

A dog's behavioral software is ultimately determined by the power of the hardware, and that means the brain. As with all animals, one of the most important determinants of brainpower is size—specifically, the size of the brain relative to the size of the body. By this measure, the human brain is huge, about one-fiftieth the mass of the average human body.

Compared with humans and their 1:50 ratio, horses are dullards, at 1:600, and lions are little better at 1:550. Dogs are comparative scholars, weighing in at an impressive 1:125—a ratio that holds across all breeds of dog, from the Chihuahua to the English mastiff. All the same, a brain that makes you a genius in the animal world is not much in the human one. Berns keeps the preserved brain of an adult German shepherd in his lab, and it starkly makes that point: the brain is the size of a tangerine. "Dog brains just don't have the real estate to do the things ours do," he says.

While the sizes of the two brains differ, the structures are strikingly similar. Over the past several years, Berns and his team have used that similarity to good effect. Much of their MRI work has focused on the part of the brain known as the striatum. Rich in dopamine, the striatum mediates reward, pleasure and expectation—three pillars of a dog's world.

During Ninja's recent visit, the experiment involved determining how quickly she would learn to expect a food reward after being exposed to one of two smells. With the scanner running, a lab assistant released intermittent puffs of either isoamyl, a chemical that smells faintly like nail-polish remover, or hexanol, a carbon molecule that is detectable in grass clippings. After each puff of isoamyl, Ninja was given a hot-dog treat; after the hexanol, she'd get nothing.

Over the course of the test, the MRI looked for upticks in electrical activity in the striatum that would indicate increased anticipation after smelling the isoamyl. Analytic software would have to determine the answer since the naked eye could not pick out such small fluctuations, but Ninja offered clues that she had learned fast. After hopping down from the scanner, she was presented with two cups in the middle of a room, each containing one of the two chemicals. She trotted straight to the one with isoamyl.

Associating a smell with a treat is basic stuff, but Berns has used his MRI to probe more sophisticated parts of dogs' cognitive prowess: how they recognize the faces of humans and other dogs; how they recognize voices and words; even how they experience jealousy–when a treat was fed in pantomime to a dog mannequin. It's those questions about a dog's personality–does it love? does it empathize? is it loyal?–that most intrigue humans.

Investigators at the Messerli Research Institute in Vienna have recently tested the ability of dogs to behave prosocially–make an effort to help another dog when there is no reward in it for them. In the experiment, two dogs were placed in side-by-side cages, and one was trained to pull a lever that would deliver food to the other. The first dog got nothing and yet was usually happy to pull the lever all the same–provided the dog on the other side was a playmate. Unknown dogs were less likely to get the same treatment.

Studies of the many ways dogs are said to come to the aid of humans have produced less positive results. There is no end of anecdotal evidence of the phenomenon: dogs that run for help when their owners are injured, dogs that bark to alert the family to a fire, dogs that know when you're sad and nuzzle to offer comfort.

Lovely–and maybe hooey. "Your dog may notice something's amiss when you're sad," says Kaminski, "but the message they're sending when they nuzzle may be 'You're acting weird, and that scares me.'" As for dogs that bark when there's a fire in the house? "They might just have been frightened," says developmental psychologist William Roberts of Ontario's Western University.

In one study Roberts and a colleague conducted, an owner walked her dog across a field and then fell to the ground, feigning a heart attack. Two other humans were seated nearby, pretending to be reading. The owner lay still for six minutes, and over repeated trials with different human and animal subjects, not a single dog sought help.

Roberts does not deny the truth of occasional stories of dogs that do seek help. But he thinks they're the exceptions. The majority of cases in which dogs do nothing "don't get reported because they are not interesting or unexpected."

If that's true, it leaves dogs as little more than, well, cats: amiable freeloaders on the human gravy train. But such a conclusion shortchanges them–by a lot.

Start with what we're learning about their intellectual octane, especially in terms of what's known as theory of mind, the ability to understand that humans and other animals have knowledge different from their own. The ability of dogs to follow pointing, and to do so innately, has generated a lot of interested in recent years. It doesn't seem like much of a skill, except when you consider that so many other animals make no sense of the gesture. The dog knows that the hand is used to indicate something else.

"When two humans do that, they take into account the common ground–a communicative context in which all this makes sense," says Kaminski. The same is true between dogs and humans.

Not all canine researchers are sold on the significance of all of this. Behavioral scientist Clive Wynne of Arizona State University cites numerous species–including dolphins, elephants and even bats–that learn the meaning of pointing if they've had sufficient exposure to human beings. "It's simply day-to-day experience with humans using their limbs to deliver things that matter," he says.

The canine understanding of object permanence is less open to dispute. Dogs perform well on so-called visible-displacement tasks: when they watch an object being placed in one of several containers and are then allowed to look for it, they know which container to investigate first. Dogs also master invisible displacement, in which, say, a toy is placed in a container, the container is moved behind a screen and then brought back out, but the toy is no longer in it. Some dogs follow that chain of events, rightly concluding that if they go behind the barrier they will probably find the toy.

In a 2013 study, behavioral psychologist Thomas Zentall of the University of Kentucky also found that dogs are capable of understanding that not only is the existence of objects permanent but so are the characteristics. When a dog biscuit or other item of interest was carried behind a barrier and then carried back out, the dogs would give it a glance as it reappeared. But if it was secretly replaced by a larger or smaller version of the same object or one that had changed in color, they would stare much longer. The conclusion: a two-inch dog biscuit should remain two inches and a yellow ball should remain yellow, and dogs understand that.

What, however, does all this say about dogs' emotional experience of the world? They exhibit what seems unmistakably to be joy–in the jumping, yipping thrill they show when family members come home after a long absence. That may even suggest that they have an awareness not just of the past and the future but also of the rate at which time passes. Closed-circuit cameras show that they seem to prepare as the time comes for humans who have been out all day to return, stirring from a nap, checking the front door, becoming restless and excited.

A sense of time as a linear thing–that the current state is not the only state–is an abstraction that human babies take a long time to learn, which partly explains tantrums. A present moment without a cookie means an eternity without cookies.

Dogs may even teach us something about a common human problem: lack of willpower. Research has attributed this to what is known as ego depletion, with self-control failing over time the same way an overworked muscle does. In studies conducted in 2010 and '15, investigators found that self-discipline in dogs breaks down the same way ours does. In one experiment, dogs that had been required to perform a 10-minute sit-and-stay exercise were less likely to complete a puzzle task given to them next than dogs that had spent the same 10 minutes doing what they pleased.

The reason may be depletion of glucose in the prefrontal cortex. Dogs given glucose before the second task stayed with it longer after a sit-and-stay period. Dosing up on sugary drinks is not the way to improve self-discipline, but the research does show us one more thing we share with our favorite nonhuman species.

Ultimately, though, our curiosity about dogs will always be driven mostly by our love for dogs. Berns believes that it was juveniles on both sides of the human-dog divide that were responsible for initiating the interspecies bond. Wolf pups would be the ones likeliest to approach and appeal to early nomadic humans; and girls and boys–then and now–are the humans who love puppies most. Dogs are like us in their joy and empathy and inexhaustible curiosity, and we–at least when we're in their presence–become more like them. We are both better species for our very long union.

8 - WHAT DOGS REALLY UNDERSTAND

What am I thinking about huh?

I t's that look that does it. Dog owners know the one. The big brown eyes open wide, the head tipped to the side with a quizzical huh? The dog wants to know what we want from them. But what is he thinking about? Does he really know when we're upset, we're sick, we're thrilled? It's a question that probably crosses a dog owner's mind every single day — but only recently have experts provided (some) answers.

A slew of new books have been published on this topic in the past couple of years, but two of the most recent stand out from the pack: Alexandra Horowitz's "Inside of a Dog: What Dogs See, Smell, and Know" (Scribner), and Jeffrey Moussaieff Masson's "The Dog Who Couldn't Stop Loving" (HarperCollins), an in-depth look at what dogs feel — namely love for their humans.

Here's what these two books and their authors reveal about what dogs know — and feel.

THE DOG'S NOSE KNOWS

"We all know dogs have good noses," Horowitz says. "But how good — that, I think, most of us don't appreciate."

Beagles can have up to 300 million smell receptors in their nose, compared to 6 million in humans. Their noses are so powerful that they can detect a teaspoon of sugar diluted in the equivalent of two Olympic-size pools full of water.

"It's only a few years ago that we discovered that dogs can sniff cancer," Masson adds. "That's pretty amazing. Their noses are still more sensitive than any machine we have, for all kinds of things."

Other things dogs can smell include fear. According to Horowitz, we sweat when under stress and dogs can smell our odor in our perspiration. They can also smell adrenaline.

They even know, it seems, what we've been up to all day. The combination of our sweat, skin cells, the odor from what we had for lunch, and traces of other bodily fluids tells dogs a whole lot more about us than we realize. According to Horowitz, "A dog knows if you've had sex, smoked a cigarette, done both these things in succession, just had a snack, or just run a mile."

Now, who still wishes their dogs could talk?

SAY WHAT? DOGS AND WORDS

While he writes extensively about his Labrador retriever Benjy's enormous capacity for love, Masson is also quick to admit that his beloved pet, a guide-dog-school dropout, is "a bit dim."

"He has a vocabulary of maybe four words," Masson says. "Things like treat and stay."

But many dogs have a much bigger vocab, or at least seem to. In her book, Horowitz cites the famous German border collie Rico, who made headlines in 2004 for his ability to identify over 200 toys by name. But border collies are the brain surgeons of the dog world, ranked first among breeds for intelligence by researchers, and Rico is unusual.

Horowitz goes on to explain how dogs, when listening to us, are really responding to sounds — and processing our babbling in conjunction with other signs and body language to work out our meaning.

Saying, "Who wants to go for a walk?" as you head to the door, for example, gives dogs a lot of clues as to what comes next. But then again, adds Horowitz, asking if your dog "wants to snow forty locks" in the same voice and you'll probably get the same reaction. A resounding, tail-wagging yes.

DOGS KNOW WHEN SOMETHING'S UP

But not necessarily that a situation is an emergency. Both Horowitz and Masson mention the experiments done by psychologists who had dog owners fake a heart attack in front of their dog to gauge their response. We've all read headlines about heroic dogs saving their owners from a house fire, or pulling children from a flooding river. But in this particular test? The dogs did not act as if the "heart attack" was an emergency. Some dogs pawed at their owners, others just wandered around in the general vicinity. In only a few instances did the dogs bark or approach a bystander who might be able to help.

Of course, as Masson points out, "Since these 'emergencies' were staged, it could well be that the dogs knew that the crises were not real."

Horowitz also explains that while dogs may not understand the concept of danger, they do know when something unusual is happening — and can be taught to respond to an emergency situation (say, in the case of a service dog alerting a deaf person to the sound of a smoke alarm).

Put simply, dogs are creatures of routine, and we only reinforce the habits. Do something out of the ordinary, and your dog will notice. But he may not call the cops to report you.

CAN DOGS TELL TIME?

In "Dogs That Know When Their Owners Are Coming Home," a 1999 book that's being updated and re-released next April, biologist Rupert Sheldrake puts forth his theory for this common occurrence — that dogs who wait patiently by the door for their owner may be relying on telepathy, a sense of direction or premonitions. But in general, little is known about how dogs do or don't watch the clock. Masson says, "I think they do have a certain sense of time. But I don't think we understand it.

"I doubt that any animal has any way of conceptualizing 'next week' or 'next year.' They have no way to know. Dogs don't think about the day after tomorrow."

ARE DOGS SELF-CENTERED?

Observe their life of couch- and bed-hogging, and thinking nothing of eating your last scrap of pumpkin pie, and it's easy to think that dogs act in service only unto themselves. But, Horowitz wonders, do dogs think about themselves? This implies that dogs have a sense of self, she explains, and it's one of her own burning questions about dog cognition that remains unanswered: "Does he reflect on his past, think about his future? Does he think about what I, or others, know?"

It turns out that in scientists' best tests of this — seeing how animals react to seeing themselves in a mirror — dogs did not score high on the self-awareness scale. Some dogs seemed to think, "Hey, who's that cute dog over there?" when seeing their reflections, while others only looked at the mirror idly.

There are other behaviors that show dogs have knowledge of themselves, however. Small dogs are purposely noisy, writes Horowitz, to compensate for their stature.

DO DOGS KNOW RIGHT FROM WRONG?

Most owners who've caught a sheepish looking pooch with his paws in the trash will say "yes!" but recent studies of dogs' expressions of guilt show interesting results. Firstly, we have to ask the question: What is prompting the look? We assume it is guilt, but Horowitz suggests that it may be something else: "the excitement of sniffing the trash or anticipation of the unhappy loud noises" that will inevitable come out of their owner.

"We assume that dogs know right and wrong, like children learn," she says. "But they are not a part of our [human] culture, and their sense of right and wrong is not going to be equivalent to ours, even though they are living in our house."

From her own experiments and those of other researchers', Horowitz says that a dog's look of guilt may actually be one of fear or submission instead — they know that an unhappy owner might mean punishment, and their expression reflects that anticipation.

DOGS SAY SORRY

If a dog unintentionally hurts a canine pal during play, he will apologize by giving a "play bow," the doggy signal that usually kicks off a play session. Masson says it's even possible that humans learned the art of apology from dogs. He also reminds us that dogs understand our apologies — when we accidentally step on their tail and say "I'm sorry" over and over again, we're usually rewarded with a lick on the hand that says "apology accepted."

Masson isn't sure why dogs don't get angry at us (aggressive dogs are usually acting out of fear). "I've often thought of it," he says, "because you can't pull that with a cat. If you do something a cat doesn't like, he'll lash out. Dogs are forgiving."

On a related note, he says, dogs don't generally go in for revenge. "I don't think there's any such thing as a sadistic dog. There are no dogs who are plotting in their mind, 'I'm going to get in this SOB.' "

This also applies to the idea some owners have of their dogs getting vengeance on them for going off to work by creating a mess in the house. "This is not vengeance," says Masson. "They just want to be with us. They don't understand why we need to separate." The mess is more likely the result of boredom.

DOGS LIVE TO LOVE

(And They Don't Leave Us)

Masson's new book is entirely devoted to this topic. Despite admitting that his beliefs wouldn't fare very well at an animal behaviorist meeting, he says, "Dogs are programmed to feel love."

When Benjy licks Masson's hand or face, he doesn't think (like the animal behaviorists) that he is soliciting food, but expressing love.

He even thinks dogs are a superior species because of how they love. "We humans leave other people," he says. "But that would never go through a dog's mind. They don't know the concept of divorce. Have you ever noticed that dogs hate to see a couple fight? They start to shake or they go under a table. They can't bear it. People have always assumed it's because they think you're going to turn on them. I don't think that's what it is. I think it's that they recognize that the love is leaking out — and that goes against their nature. They smell love gone sour, and they don't like it."

The flip side of that coin is that dogs enjoy watching love flow around them. "Whenever I kiss my wife, Benjy's tail starts thumping on the floor," says Masson. "He just loves it. It's like he's saying, 'That's the way! You got it! More of that!' "

WHAT'S NEXT?

As much as we do know about dogs, there's so much more we don't. And some of our knowledge falls into a grey area: dogs are said to dream and laugh — but in their own ways. More study is needed to fully understand these behaviors.

"Right now we're testing whether dogs have a sense of fairness," Horowitz says. "The results are still out!"

But as the researchers do their jobs, dog owners can do theirs by learning how their dog experiences the world. "You'll have the best relationship with your dog if you understand what he knows," she says. "If you realize how much of his world smelling is, you'll see his sniffing everything as just 'looking at the world,' not as slowing you down. And if you spend a moment imagining the world from two feet off the ground, you see that it's no surprise when dogs jump up at us — our mouths, smelling of food, are so far away!"

THREE THINGS YOUR DOG WANTS YOU TO KNOW:

SWITCH TO DIGITAL TV!

She is so beautiful <3

While some dogs have been known to stare at the screen when it's tuned to Animal Planet, they're not known for getting sucked into hours in front of the tube. That's because dogs have a higher flicker-fusion rate than humans do, writes Alexandra Horowitz in "Inside of a Dog." TV fools human eyes into seeing a continuous stream of images (rather than the reality: a sequence of stills) but it's not fast enough for dogs, so they wind up seeing individual frames and the dark spaces between them. Not exactly must-see TV. The conversion to digital broadcasts, however, will eliminate the flicker-fusion problem.

THEY DON'T LIKE RAINCOATS

Dogs already have a coat, Horowitz points out. And the feeling of a raincoat being placed on their back might feel like it does when another dog stands over and dominates them. "The be-jacketed dog may cooperate in going out," she writes, "but not because he has shown he likes the coat; it is because he has been subdued."

YOU DON'T NEED TO BE THE ALPHA DOG

Sorry, Cesar Millan. Horowitz says that pet owners who've gobbled up all that "pack leader" talk are barking up the wrong tree. "Wolves in the wild live in family units, and the young wolves don't compete to become alpha," she says. In other words, it's wrong to think that dogs are vying to be the leader of our packs or families when we bring them home. "We absolutely do not need to dominate them," says Horowitz. Positive reinforcement works just as well.

13 REVEALING SECRETS YOUR DOG KNOWS ABOUT YOU

Dogs notice when you're sad, mad, or suspicious. They can even detect cancer. Turns out, dogs know more about your emotions and health than you ever suspected. Below are what dogs know about you.

1. YOU'RE A GENEROUS PERSON (OR NOT)

I make judgments about you based on your actions. University of Milan researchers had dogs watch some people sharing food with a beggar and other people telling the beggar to leave. Later, when the individuals beckoned the dogs at the same time, the pups overwhelmingly trotted over to the generous people.

2. YOU DON'T LIKE SOMEONE

When you have negative feelings about a person, I can hear your breathing pattern change, observe your body stiffen slightly, and even smell the subtle pheremones your body emits. So if your in-laws suspect that I don't like them, it may simply be because, um, you don't really like them. Speaking of smells, this is why your dog's breath smells so bad.

3. WHERE YOU'VE BEEN

You humans are like sponges. You pick up volatile organic compounds from everything you walk by or touch. If you just visited, say, the supermarket, I will smell the butcher and fish counters, the food you bought, and maybe even the people you stood next to at checkout. I can smell something 100 million times more subtle than the faintest smell you can pick up.

4. YOU MAY HAVE CANCER

Some of us are being taught to detect different types of cancer by smelling certain chemicals that cancer cells can emit. In some studies, we were 88 percent accurate in detecting breast cancer, and 99 percent accurate in detecting lung cancer.

5. YOU'RE COMING HOME

We've learned your schedule, and we know roughly when to expect you back at the house each day. But even if you an get home at an odd hour, I can pick out the sound of your particular car coming down the street, and I am always listening for it.

6. YOU'VE HAD A FIGHT WITH YOUR SPOUSE

Even if you don't yell in front of me, I may notice your clipped tone of voice, the fact that neither of you is speaking, the stiffness of your posture, or the agitated way you're walking or opening drawers. Some of us get sick to our stomachs when our owners are bickering.

7. YOU NEED PROTECTION

Do I sleep cuddled up next to your bed instead of in my usual spot when your spouse is out of town? Do I stay closer to your leg than normal when we walk through a dark area? I can smell the adrenaline your body releases when you're scared, and I'm also more vigilant anytime someone in the household is missing. These are the 8 sure signs that your dog trusts you.

8. YOU'RE GOING ON A TRIP

I hate it when you leave, so I've learned to pick up on all the clues when a departure is imminent–suitcases pulled from the closet or the way you always spread clothes out on your bed. Some of us start to shake and pant because our anxiety spikes. Feel bad? One study found playing classical music for us when we're alone can help us calm down. Make sure you avoid these mistakes every dog owner makes.

9. YOU'RE A SUCKER FOR OUR PUPPY DOG EYES

Researchers have found that your body releases the hormone oxytocin (the same chemical that's released when you look at your baby) when we make eye contact with you. So there's a reason we gaze at you lovingly when we want something: It works.

10. WHAT YOUR INTENTIONS ARE

I can pick up nearly imperceptible signals in your body language—a darting of your eyes or the way you grab the leash—that tell me what you're planning. In one study, dogs were easily able to identify the location of hidden food simply by following a human gaze.

11. YOU'RE NOT FEELING WELL

We can be trained to sniff out everything from a drop in your blood sugar to a migraine. A growing number of epileptic patients are getting dogs that alert them to a seizure before it happens. In one Hawaiian hospital, dogs sniffed out urinary tract infections in paralyzed patients who couldn't report symptoms.

12. YOUR BABY IS WEAK

I know your little one is a member of my pack, and I also know she's the most vulnerable. Because I have a strong instinct to guard my family members, I can be extremely protective. That's why I bark aggressively when someone approaches the stroller and why you should be vigilant if someone is playing with your child while I'm around. (If I mistakenly think she is getting hurt, I may attack.)

13. YOU'RE BUMMED OUT

I am a master at reading your body language and emotional state. One study found that I can tell if someone's sad simply by reading facial expressions (even if I'm looking at a photo of just half a face!). I'm also more likely to approach someone who is crying than someone humming or talking, an indication of empathy. Next, find out the 30 things your dog wishes you knew.

Sometimes I'm kind of silly, but I know all about you..

9 - DOGS' BRAIN PROBLEMS

Oops, my friends are checking up, too!!

As in humans, a dog's brain and nervous system are very complex. Learn about dog neural health, possible diseases and issues, and what you can do.

The nervous system of a dog is comprised of the dog's brain, spinal cord, and the nerves traveling between the two and throughout your dog's body. The nervous system controls a dog's actions, from movement to play to eating and to emotional behavior. A dog's neurological disorder can occur as a result of external factors like an injury, a reaction to medication, hereditary diseases, or general health problems. Find out some common neurological problems that can impact dogs, as well as some breed-specific disorders to watch for.

EPILEPSY IN DOGS

Perhaps one of the most well-known neurological disorders is epilepsy, which is characterized by recurrent seizures. Epilepsy can be caused by trauma, like a head injury, or metabolic issues, but the causes can also commonly be idiopathic, meaning that veterinarians are not quite sure why the dog has the disease. Treatment of epilepsy is aimed at reducing how long the seizures last and how frequently they take place. While the seizures can be quite scary, the day-to-day quality of life for a dog with epilepsy often remains high.

HEREDITARY DISEASES IN DOG BREEDS

Some neurological problems are the result of inherited conditions; with careful breeding, these kind of diseases can often be avoided.

Dancing Doberman Disease: This disease affects Dobermans only, and causes the gastrocnemius muscle, located in the dog's legs, to flex and extend. Dogs will eventually avoid standing entirely to avoid this uncontrollable movement. Both males and females can get this disease.

Scottie Cramp: As with Dancing Doberman Disease, Scottie Cramp is a disease that impacts a dog's legs. Only affecting Scottish Terriers, this disease is carried by a recessive gene, and can be eliminated through proper breeding. Scottish Terriers that have this disease will hyperextend and hyperflex their legs, and experience leg spasms.

NEURAL DISEASES ASSOCIATED WITH DOG BREEDS

Some neural diseases, while not necessarily hereditary in nature, are closely associated with specific breeds of dogs.

White Dog Shaker Syndrome: While not exclusively experienced by dogs with white fur, a large number of dogs with this syndrome are white. The causes of the disease are unknown. Dogs with this condition shake and tremble. Corticosteroids can be used as a treatment method if the causes are neurological in nature.

Cauda Equina Syndrome: Also known as Lumbosacral stenosis, this arthritic condition occurs in a dog's hind legs. It's quite painful, especially when dogs lie down, and dogs can also have have trouble urinating or defecating as a result. Cauda Equina syndrome occurs because of a narrowing in the dog's spinal column, and can be easily confused with hip dysplasia. Large breeds, especially German Shepherds and Greyhounds, are most commonly afflicted.

ACQUIRED NEURAL DISEASES

These diseases, which greatly impact a dog's neurological system, are characterized as being caught from other dogs or animals, or acquired through exposure.

Tick Paralysis: All ticks are problematic, but some females will transmit poison to dogs during the biting process, which will cause paralysis and breathing difficulties. These nervous system problems will occur within a few days of the bite, and with the removal of the tick, the symptoms will generally dissipate. In some cases, hospitalization will be required.

Distemper: This virus is highly contagious, and attacks the brain cells and skin cells of dogs. It's most common in younger dogs and symptoms usually begin with respiratory issues that progress to anorexia, lethargy, abnormal coloring in the eyes, and sometimes seizures. Vaccines can prevent distemper, but recovery once the disease is contracted is rare.

Rabies: Another virus, rabies is caught from bites from other animals with rabies, and attacks your dog's nervous system. Rabies is a serious disease, and your pet will need to be quarantined -- even if they were vaccinated in the past. (A vaccine will decrease the duration of the quarantine, however.)

OTHER MAJOR NEUROLOGICAL DISEASES IN DOGS

As well as the diseases mentioned above, some other common neurological diseases and conditions that can occur in dogs are:

Facial Nerve Paralysis: As is apparent from this condition's name, muscles in the face will become paralyzed as the result of either the symptom of another disease or for unknown reasons. Although there isn't a specific treatment, treatment of the underlying disease can resolve the situation. Many dogs will recover on their own.

Wobbler Disease: This disease affects the cervical spine -- you'll recognize it by the dog's wobbling walking movements. Surgery is one treatment option.

Parkinson's Disease: As with people, Parkinson's disease has symptoms of tremors and difficulty walking, and is unfortunately incurable. Medications can help reduce symptoms somewhat. With people, this disease develops relatively late in life, but dogs can get this degenerative disease at a relatively young age.

Given the vital role that the nervous system plays in your dog's behavior, many diseases can cause dogs to display neurological symptoms, such as tremors, seizures, or paralysis. If you notice these kinds of movement-related symptoms, or a major shift in your dog's behavior, take your dog to the veterinarian for a check-up.

10 - A TYPICAL DAILY ROUTINE FOR A DOG OR PUPPY

I'm hungry.. Is it time to eat??

07:00 - Dogs like to go to the toilet as soon as they wake up, so make sure that you go outside with him as soon as you come downstairs. Introduce a bit of playtime once he has done his business, and maybe bring a couple of his favourite toys out with you to keep his attention.

07.30 - If you have decided to feed your dog two meals a day, this is the perfect time to give him his breakfast. This is also the best time to feed your dog his first meal of the day.

08.00 - About half an hour after your dog has finished eating, take him outside for a brisk walk and another opportunity to go to the toilet. Typically dogs like to go to the toilet between 10 and 30 minutes after they have eaten. Adult dogs are better at holding it in, but puppies can really struggle.

09.00 - This is when you either allow your dog to settle and rest just before you leave for work, or allow him to explore and amuse himself with some interactive toys as you get things done.

13.00 - Ideally, most dogs would love for you to return home during your lunch break so that they can be let out to go to the toilet and spend some quality time exercising, playing and bonding with you. Replace your dog's water for a fresh clean bowl. If you have a puppy, this is the best time to give him his midday meal.

13.30 - Before you head back to work, make sure that you take your dog outside to relieve himself, otherwise you might be presented with a little treat when you arrive home. Encourage your dog to use some energy by introducing some play (and training if you have enough time), and then invite him back inside to calm down and rest - a crate is the most effective way of teaching a dog to calm down after exercise. To find out how to correctly crate train a dog or puppy follow this link to our crate training section.

17.00 - As soon as your return home from work, offer your dog a fresh, clean bowl of water. Now is also the best time to give your puppy or older dog his evening meal. Shortly after he has finished eating, take him outside to use all of the energy he has built up throughout the day. You can use this time to do some training - training to fetch, heel, come/recall, sit, stay, lie down.

19.00 - Your dog will want to relieve himself one more time before he goes to bed. Take him outside to go to the toilet, but don't offer any play. You dont want to get him too excited, otherwise you might struggle to get him to settle for bedtime. As you invite your pup back inside, reward calm behaviour so that he knows that it is time to rest. The most effective method of teaching a dog to calm or settle is crate training.

11 - 65 WAYS TO BE A RESPONSIBLE DOG OWNER

Living with my boss.. is my happiness <3

Owning a dog is a joy, privilege, and responsibility. If you are considering bringing a canine companion into your life, think seriously about the commitment that being a responsible dog owner entails.

The AKC is committed to protecting the health and well-being of all dogs. In honor of AKC's Responsible Dog Ownership Day, here are 75 tips on how to be a good dog owner.

PREPARE TO BE A RESPONSIBLE DOG OWNER

1. Recognize the commitment

Before deciding that a dog is right for you, make an honest assessment: are you ready for the financial, emotional, and time commitment owning a dog requires?

2. Evaluate your lifestyle

Think about the type of dog that will best suit your lifestyle. Evaluate all aspects of your family's life — hobbies, activities, personalities — before choosing a breed.

3. Make a list

Based on your evaluation, what qualities do you want in a dog? Consider size, energy level, grooming needs, trainability, and temperament. If you rent an apartment, are there restrictions on height, weight, or breed? Answer these questions now, because once you bring a dog home, it can be heartbreaking to realize you made the wrong choice.

4. Choose a breed

Once you have made your list of ideal characteristics, do some research to find out which breeds fit that profile. Read up, attend dog shows, and visit AKC's breed pages.

5. Get referrals to responsible breeders

You have a better chance of success if you get your dog from a responsible, ethical breeder. The AKC has a Breeder Referral contact for each recognized breed. They can put you in touch with breeders or rescue organizations in your area.

6. Contact breeders

Reach out to breeders in your area. Don't be discouraged if the first breeder you talk to doesn't have puppies available right away. That person may know of another breeder in the region.

7. Ask questions

When you find a breeder you're comfortable with, ask to visit the kennel and view the dogs on the breeder's premises. Don't be afraid to ask questions about the breed and the breeder's practices.

8. Consider an older dog

Puppies aren't for everyone. If an older dog better fits your lifestyle, check the AKC Rescue Network. Most rescue dogs have been spayed or neutered and are screened for health and temperament issues.

9. Expect questions

A responsible breeder or rescue organization will ask you extensive questions about the type of home you can offer a dog. They are as committed as you to making the right match.

10. Prepare to wait for the perfect dog

Availability varies. Responsible breeders do not breed often, and many times the puppies of a planned breeding are already spoken for. A good dog is worth waiting for.

11. Skip the holidays

Most breeders don't recommend giving dogs as a present. A new puppy needs your undivided attention, which is difficult during the holiday season. A better idea is to give dog-related gifts — toys, leashes, grooming tools — and then bring your puppy home when all of the excitement has died down.

COMMIT TO DOG OWNERSHIP

12. Choose your dog

Listen to your breeder's suggestions about which puppy in the litter is right for you. If you are rescuing an older dog, get input from the rescue organization.

13. Get it in writing

Information about the sale or adoption should be in writing. The contract should include details about fees, spay-neuter agreements, health guarantees, terms of co-ownership, restrictions on breeding, and living arrangements. It should also include instructions on what to do if the dog, despite your best efforts, simply doesn't work out for you or your family. Most responsible breeders will insist that the dog be returned to them.

14. Get your papers

You should receive an AKC registration application from your breeder when you purchase the puppy. Make sure the breeder completes the appropriate sections of the form and signs it. The breeder can also help you fill out your section correctly.

15. Register your dog

Send your completed application to the AKC. Your dog will then become part of the nation's largest registry of purebred dogs. If you rescue a dog, consider applying for a Purebred Alternative Listing/Indefinite Listing Privilege (PAL/ILP) number. This allows your dog to participate in some performance events.

GET READY TO BRING YOUR NEW DOG HOME

16. Buy the necessities…and toys.

Purchase food, treats, a collar and leash, toys, grooming tools, and other things you'll need in advance so that your dog or puppy's transition into your home will be a smooth one.

17. Make a schedule

You and your family members should decide who will be responsible for food, water, walks, exercise, cleanup, and grooming. Post a schedule of tasks to remind everyone of their responsibilities.

KEEP YOUR DOG HEALTHY

18. Schedule regular check-ups

The AKC provides 30 days of pet insurance coverage from AKC Pet Insurance for newly registered puppies. Details about this complimentary benefit will be sent to you shortly after registration.

19. Feed him a healthy diet

Your breeder or vet can suggest food that is best for your dog's age, size, and activity level. Keep the diet consistent. Always provide plenty of fresh, clean water.

20. Exercise

Take your dog for walks, play games, run in the yard, throw a ball around — anything to stimulate his mind and body.

21. Vaccinate

Make sure your dog is up-to-date on his vaccinations and keep a copy of his records handy.

22. Prevent disease

Depending on where you live, your dog could be at risk for diseases like heartworm and Lyme disease. Ask your vet for prevention tips.

23. Repel fleas and ticks

Keep your dog, his bedding, and your home free from parasites.

24. Know your dog's patterns

You will become familiar with your dog's patterns of eating, drinking, sleeping, and relieving himself. Any major variations in these patterns could indicate illness.

25. Bathe your dog

Wash your dog with shampoo meant for canines. How often you should wash him will depend on his breed and environment. If this task is too overwhelming for you, take him to a groomer or vet.

26. Groom your dog

Some short-coated breeds need just a quick brushing every week, while some longer-coated breeds need daily brushing to prevent matting and reduce shedding.

27. Clip those nails

Learn how to clip your dog's nails or have the vet or groomer do it.

28. Clean those teeth

To prevent tooth decay and gum disease, clean your dog's teeth regularly. You can also give him hard biscuits, rope bones, or nylon chews to help keep them clean.

29. Keep your dog fit and trim

Feed him a well-balanced diet and give him plenty of exercise. Don't overdo it with the treats.

30. Know the breed's health risks

You should be aware of common health problems, how to prevent them, and how to recognize their onset.

31. Be alert to changing needs

As your dog ages, his needs will change. He may require a different diet, need more sleep, and be less active. You should do everything you can to pamper him in his final years.

32. Know when to let go

If, due to illness or old age, your dog reaches a point where his quality of life is severely compromised, arrange to end his life humanely.

KEEP YOUR DOG SAFE

33. ID your dog

He should wear an identification tag with your name, address, and phone number at all times.

34. Get your dog microchipped

Microchips are a way to permanently identify your dog, and can be invaluable in recovering a lost canine companion. Consider enrolling your dog in AKC Reunite, which is the nation's largest database of microchipped pets.

35. Travel safely

Keep your dog safe in the car by using a crate or seat belt harness.

36. Prepare for a disaster

Have a disaster plan in place. Make an emergency kit with clean water, food, and first aid equipment. Find out in advance if evacuation shelters in your area allow animals.

37. Establish an emergency contact

Enlist a family member or friend, ideally someone your dog knows, to take care of him in case of illness, hospitalization, or other emergencies. Leave a list of general care instructions in a safe place.

BE YOUR DOG'S FRIEND

38. Play

Set aside time each day for play sessions. It's fun, provides an outlet for your pup's energy, and strengthens the bond between you.

39. Take walks

Your dog will enjoy exploring the neighborhood and he'll benefit from the exercise.

40. Talk to your dog

Your canine companion won't understand your words, but he will enjoy the sound of your voice. You can also use different voice levels to praise or correct your dog's behavior.

41. Give treats

Your dog will always appreciate a treat, which also serves as an excellent training aid.

42. Switch out toys

Keep your dog entertained by rotating his toys. Put "old" toys out of sight for a month or two and then bring them back out again.

43. Plan activities and trips with your dog

Include your dog in family activities. Take him to the park, beach, or to special activities such as a dog parade. If you're traveling to an event, check ahead for lodging that accepts dogs. If you're flying, ask about travel accommodations for your dog when you make the reservation.

44. Give him a massage

Recent studies have shown that massages may be beneficial to your dog's health and behavior.

45. Ease separation anxiety

Help your dog get used to being alone. Leave him each day with a minimum amount of fuss. When you come home, greet him calmly. This will teach him that you leaving is not something to be concerned about.

TRAIN YOUR DOG

46. Teach basic commands

Teach your dog basic commands such as sit, stay, come, and down. Training your dog makes your life easier, fulfills his desire to please you, and strengthens your bond.

47. Socialize Your Dog

Expose your dog to different people and settings regularly. Take him to the park, to the pet store, on a walk through town. Praise him for behaving calmly around strangers and other dogs.

48. Go to class

Obedience classes can be a great experience for you and your dog. You may even discover that your dog has a talent for obedience, agility, or other AKC sports.

49. Praise your dog

Praise him lavishly for obeying commands and behaving well. Using positive, rather than negative, reinforcement will help your dog enjoy training.

50. Supervise play with children

Children and dogs can be great friends, but they need supervision when playing together, no matter how friendly your canine companion might be.

51. Give your dog a job

Teach him to fetch the paper or carry groceries. Giving your dog a sense of purpose and accomplishment increases his well being.

BREED RESPONSIBLY

52. Breed to improve

Breeding should only be done for the advancement of the breed. If you are thinking about breeding your dog, consult your breeder for advice.

53. Contain bitches in heat

Males can sense a female in heat up to five miles away. If your female dog goes into heat, keep her properly secured.

54. Do genetic screening

If you plan to breed your dog, it is very important to test for health and disease. Perform all available tests to rule out the possibility of passing on a genetic defect.

GET INVOLVED

55. Join an AKC club

Many clubs offer educational seminars and health clinics. It's also a good place to start if you plan to participate in competitive events with your dog.

56. Earn an AKC title

Explore the world of dog sports by participating in AKC events. The AKC offers titles for accomplishment over a wide range of levels. Find an event that's right for your dog and have fun.

57. Encourage breed behavior

Find activities that will encourage your dog to fulfill his breed's purpose. The AKC offers many performance events geared toward specific breeds.

58. Involve the kids

Your children can learn more about dogs and dog care by participating in AKC Junior Showmanship events. Through the National Junior Organization, your child can compete in conformation and performance events, attend seminars, and even earn scholarships.

59. Find a mentor

If you plan to breed or show your dog, find an experienced person in the breed to show you the ropes. A mentor can make your "novice" days much easier.

60. Read all about it

Keep up with the latest dog news by reading AKC publications. From "The Complete Dog Book" to the AKC Gazette to numerous free publications, the AKC provides a wealth of materials on all areas of the dog world.

BE A CANINE AMBASSADOR

61. Set a good example

As a dog owner, you are responsible not only for your own dog's well being, but for the status of dogs everywhere. Owning a friendly, clean, well-mannered dog reflects positively on the species.

62. Respect your neighbors

Not everyone will love your dog as much as you do. Keep your dog on your property. Don't force your dog's company on a neighbor who isn't comfortable with dogs.

63. Fight anti-dog legislation

Be a voice against legislation directed against specific breeds. For more information, contact the Government Relations and Public Education departments at the AKC.

64. Get a Canine Good Citizen Certificate

Your dog can become an AKC Canine Good Citizen by passing a test designed to demonstrate good manners and acceptable behavior in everyday situations. The CGC program has become a standard for recognizing obedient dogs and responsible dog owners throughout the country.

65. Show your pride

Bringing a well-behaved dog into public places or showing off his talents at competitive events is an excellent way to "advertise" the rewards of canine companionship.

While no means exhaustive, these 65 steps will set you up to be a responsible dog owner.